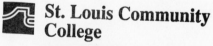

Women Today

*L*eaders

by
Cecilia Fannon

The Rourke Corporation, Inc.
Vero Beach, Florida 32964

Whatever women do, they must do twice as well as men to be thought half as good. Luckily, this is not difficult.
—Charlotte Whitton
Former Mayor of Ottawa, Canada

The Rourke Corporation, Inc.
P.O. Box 3328, Vero Beach, FL 32964

Fannon, Cecilia, 1950-
    Leaders/ by Cecilia Fannon.
        p. cm. —(Women today)
    Includes bibliographical references and index.
    Summary: Capsule biographies of prominent women in such fields as politics, science, religion, business, and literature.
    ISBN 0-86593-118-6
    1. Feminists—Biography—Juvenile literature.   2. Women in politics—Biography—Juvenile literature.   3. Women in public life—Biography—Juvenile literature.   4. Women and religion—Biography—Juvenile literature.   5. Women in science—Biography—Juvenile literature   6. Women educators—Biography—Juvenile literature.   7. Women in business—Biography—Juvenile literature.
8. Women authors—Biography—Juvenile literature.   9. Women and the military—Biography—Juvenile literature.   10. Policewomen—Biography—Juvenile literature.
[1. Women—Biography] I. Title   II. Series
HQ1154.F275   1991
305.4'092'2—dc20   91-11570
[B]   CIP
                                                                                  AC

Series Editor: Elizabeth Sirimarco
Editors: Gregory Lee, Marguerite Aronowitz
Book design and production: The Creative Spark, Capistrano Beach, California
Cover Photograph: Bob Daemmrich/The Image Works

Contents

Introduction

Women around the world are working—inside the home and out—but often for little or no pay. The work they do is mostly traditional or gender-specific to the part of the world in which they live. For example, most African and Southeast Asian women do farming, and women in the United States still do most of the bank clerking, primary school teaching, and nursing. Cultural stereotyping and lack of female role models can keep women doing the "women's work" they have done for centuries.

In the past two decades, however, this picture has changed, particularly in Europe and the United States. Laws have helped women get nontraditional employment and more equal pay. Governments are beginning to bow to world scrutiny and pass laws protecting women's rights. But many barriers to women's advancement still remain, barriers that might take as long as a century to overcome.

The inroads women have made into government, science, the military, and business must not be ignored. This book describes 24 of these women whose ideas, talent and leadership have and will continue to reshape world history.

1 Pioneers Of Feminism

In the late 1960s and early 1970s, a women's revolution took place. The goal of many women was and still is equality with men, their rightful share in the economy, and access to power. The new name applied to the movement was *feminism*, but the idea was hardly new. As far back as the 6th century, Empress Theodora of Byzantium recognized the rights of women when she passed strict divorce and anti-prostitution laws.

Centuries later in 1872, the British writer Mary Wollstonecraft wrote "A Vindication of the Rights of Women" in which she pleaded for the higher education of women. Elizabeth Cady Stanton organized the 1848 women's rights convention in Seneca Falls, New York—the first organized demand for women's suffrage.

In 1928, a British novelist named Virginia Woolf wrote an essay called "A Room of One's Own," in which she asked why men have always had power, influence, wealth and fame, while women have had nothing but children. Woolf and women of her time were the forerunners of the feminist movement.

In France in 1949, another woman, Simone de Beauvoir, wrote a book called *The Second Sex*. In it, de Beauvoir argued that "women are not born, but made." She passionately wanted to get rid of the myth of the "eternal feminine." Interestingly enough, her ideas ignited the fire of equality not so much in French women, but in American women. Fifteen years later the women's liberation movement in the United States began. Questions women had been asking for centuries were repeated in the 1960s and 1970s. Only this time, more people were listening and ready to give answers.

Since then, governments around the world have passed laws to protect women's rights, punish domestic violence, and establish child care programs. More women today work at better jobs than ever before. They are athletes, politicians, heads of government, U.S. Marines, and clergy. Women's achievements of the last 25 years would not have been possible had it not been for the seeds of change planted by the feminist movement.

Betty Friedan

In 1963, a newly published book catapulted its author into the American spotlight. The author was Betty Friedan and the book was called *The Feminine Mystique*. In it Friedan described in detail the unsatisfying lives led by American housewives. She also laid bare the many myths surrounding the notion of ideal womanhood, that is, as housewife and mother. Friedan maintained that American women should join their male counterparts in society and in the workplace.

Peoria, Illinois, was the birthplace of Elizabeth Naomi Goldstein (Betty Friedan) in 1921. Friedan grew up in an upper middle-class family. Her father owned a jewelry store and her mother was active in community affairs. From the first, Betty was an avid reader and excellent student. She attended Smith College and majored in psychology.

After graduation, Betty had a psychology fellowship at the University of California at Berkeley. Deciding against going for a Ph.D., she moved instead to New York City and wrote for a labor newspaper, *Federated Press*. In New York she also met and married Carl Friedan in 1947. Friedan took a year off after the birth of her first child, but then returned to work to write freelance articles for women's magazines.

In 1957, as a project for her 15th college reunion,

Betty Friedan helped found the National Organization for Women (NOW), and was a pioneer in the feminist movement beginning in the 1960s.

Friedan questioned her former classmates, asking them if they were happy with their lives. To her surprise, they were overwhelmingly dissatisfied. After she decided to expand her results into a book and published *The Feminine Mystique* in 1963, a female revolution began. The book said women were wasting their lives by staying at home, and that they should be in the workplace in equal force with men. The book reached more than three million readers and was translated into 13 languages. In 1966 she and other activists formed the

National Organization for Women (NOW), whose main goal was and continues to be stopping discrimination in the workplace. Their first big achievement was convincing newspapers to discontinue segregating help wanted ads by gender.

In 1971 Friedan led the first National Women's Political Caucus, which helped elect Bella Abzug to Congress. She supported the Equal Rights Amendment (ERA) that was meant to be added to the U.S. Constitution. The ERA stated "Equality of rights under the law shall not be denied or abridged by the United States or by any State on account of sex." The amendment did not pass, however, because only 35 of the necessary 38 states approved it.

Today Betty Friedan continues to champion equal rights for women and senior citizens. She speaks at demonstrations, writes articles and books, and leads rallies to support her causes. She has changed the thinking patterns and prejudices of both men and women, and plans to continue to be a pioneer for equal rights well into the next century.

Gloria Steinem

Perhaps the most visible American feminist during the 1970s and 1980s was Gloria Steinem, founder of *Ms.* magazine. She supported Shirley Chisholm, the first black woman to run for President, and was one of the planners of the 1977 National Women's Conference in Houston.

Gloria Steinem was born in Toledo, Ohio, in March 1934. Her parents were financially affected by the Great Depression and drifted from state to state in search of employment. Her father, an unsuccessful businessman, left home when Gloria was 10 and her sister was away at college. She cared for her ailing mother until she left for Smith College. There she studied political science and wrote articles on politics for the school paper.

After graduating with honors from Smith in 1956,

A founding editor of *Ms.* magazine is Gloria Steinem, a popular author who has chronicled the feminist movement for 25 years.

she traveled to India for a two-year fellowship. The Indian subcontinent intrigued her so much that she wrote a book about her experiences. She saw first-hand how different social customs affected and oppressed women around the world.

In 1960 Steinem moved to New York where she became a freelance journalist. Three years later she wrote an article called "A Bunny's Tale" that caused a sensation. Under an assumed name, Steinem had worked for three weeks as a Playboy bunny in the Manhattan Club to gather information for her article. After she wrote about the exploitation of women workers there, she received numerous freelance writing assignments and greater visibility.

By 1968 Steinem had helped co-found *New York* magazine, to which she contributed articles on politics, peace rallies, and returning Vietnam veterans. The following year, she wrote her first feminist article, "After Black Power, Women's Liberation." From that time on, she was at the forefront of the women's movement.

Working women, in particular, identified with Steinem when she wrote about job and gender discrimination. *Time* magazine published Steinem's essay, "What It Would Be Like if Women Win," in which Steinem described how women are discriminated against in every aspect of their lives. Such outspoken views brought her more and more national recognition.

The largest women's rights demonstration—held in various cities nationwide—was organized by Steinem. The Women's Strike for Equality was held on August 26, 1970—exactly 50 years since women had won the right to vote. The goal of the strike was to secure job and education equality for women, free child care, and the right to abortions for women who wanted them. In 1971 she helped found *Ms.* magazine, the National Women's Political Caucus, and the Women's Action Alliance.

Steinem continues to write on various topics such as the meaning of work, the different thinking patterns of men and women, and politics. As the 21st century approaches, Gloria Steinem's writing will undoubtedly continue to challenge society and inspire future generations to strive for equality.

2 Politics And Government

Women as world leaders is not a recent phenomenon. Cleopatra was queen of Egypt from 51 to 30 B.C. Boadicea ruled Britain early in the first century A.D. Empress Theodora of Byzantium, wife of the emperor Justinian I who reigned from 527-565, was considered the most powerful woman in Byzantine history. Queen Elizabeth I ruled England from 1558 to 1603. Catherine the Great was Empress of Russia from 1762 to 1796. Queen Victoria of England ruled for 64 years, from 1837 to 1901, and Tz'u-hsi, Dowager Empress of China, presided for 50 years over the Manchu dynasty until its fall in 1908. Queen Liliuokalani led the Hawaiian Islands from 1891-1893. And these are but a few of the women who have ruled countries and continents throughout history.

Internationally, women have achieved the highest offices in several countries: Indira Gandhi of India, Golda Meir of Israel, Margaret Thatcher of Great Britain, Queen Elizabeth II of Great Britain, Benazir Bhutto of Pakistan, Corazon Aquino of the Philippines, Kazimiera Prunskiene of Lithuania, and Mary Robinson of Ireland. In the crumbling dictatorships of third world countries and emerging democracies of Eastern and central Europe, women are making history by taking chief roles in their countries' governments.

Amazingly, American women's equality in government lags behind their Asian and European counterparts, but they are starting to make a dent. About 14 percent of the United States Congress is women, and many states and cities have elected women governors and mayors. However, women continue to have a difficult time financing campaigns in male-dominated funding circles. The American public still believes that certain issues appeal more to women. For example, women stand for the environment, education, and abortion, while men run on military issues and the economy. For women seeking high offices, the "glass ceiling"—the invisible barrier that keeps women from attaining their goals— remains to be shattered.

Violeta Chamorro

In February 1990 the people of Nicaragua voted Violeta Chamorro as their country's first woman president. The elections were open and competitive, representing another first for Nicaragua. For a decade this Central American country had been involved in a deadly civil war. When Chamorro took office, she vowed there would be peace. She kept her word. Peacefully disarming the Contra force, she reduced the ranks of the rival Sandinista force by two-thirds. In a symbolic ceremony in September 1990, 15,000 Contra rebel rifles were dumped into a trench dug next to a Managuan highway, covered with roses, and cemented over. On this spot President Chamorro hopes to someday build a monument to peace.

Born in 1930 to a wealthy family in southern Nicaragua, Chamorro has lived a privileged life compared to most Nicaraguan women. One of seven children, she attended a Catholic school in San Antonio, Texas, and Blackstone College in Virginia. Before completing her college education, however, she returned to Nicaragua where she later married outspoken newspaper publisher Pedro Joaquin Chamorro. He actively opposed the military government with a powerful voice that the government would not tolerate. Finally he was imprisoned, exiled, and shot to death. His death in 1978 marked the beginning of Nicaragua's civil war. The following year, when the country's leader fled, Violeta Chamorro took

President Violeta Chamorro was elected president of Nicaragua in February 1990 after years of civil war and martial law under the *Sandinistas*.

over her husband's spot on the newspaper *La Prensa*, and backed the Contras' cause.

Although she fast became the most popular opposition figure in Nicaragua, she stayed away from politics until 1990 when she was elected President. Today she is the national symbol of healing and peace and has brought about the end to the civil war. But she still has a difficult task: healing Nicaragua's economy. Nicaragua has an exceedingly high inflation rate and 40 percent unemployment. No one knows if President Chamorro can control the runaway inflation or lead the nation to economic stability. Only one year into her presidency, she has already brought peace to this war-torn land and restored its people's faith in free expression and enterprise. Hopefully the courageous woman who has united a divided Nicaragua can find the solutions needed to cure the nation's economic ills as well.

Gro Harlem Brundtland

Gro (pronounced GREW) Harlem Brundtland first became Prime Minister of Norway in 1981. She served for only eight months, but then returned to power from 1986 to 1989. During the past decade Brundtland has helped appoint women to many government positions. The Norwegian Parliament is currently more than one-third female, and the 17-member cabinet is made up of 50 percent female ministers.

It is Brundtland's political and economic accomplishments, however, that make her an internationally acclaimed leader. In 1986 Norway was deep in debt due to a collapse in world oil prices. Brundtland put a cap on salaries, devalued the *krone* (Norway's currency) and put restrictions on consumer credit to restore Norway's export markets. She also did not neglect the needs of Norwegian workers. She reduced the work week by several hours and extended paid maternity leave to 24 weeks.

Brundtland comes from a political family who encouraged her to set high personal goals. Her father was a doctor and Labor Party Defense Minister; her mother, a civil servant. At age seven Brundtland joined the Labor Party's Association for Juniors where she received early training in social and civic duties. She remained active in Labor Party activities through college. Like her father, she wanted to become a doctor. After receiving her medical degree from the University of Oslo, she attended Harvard's School of Public Health. During this time she married Arne Brundtland, a journalist. They have four children.

In October 1984 the United Nations appointed Brundtland to chair a commission on the environment. As a result, she wrote the "Brundtland Report," a document that brought world attention to the deteriorating world environment. This report called for increased international concern for the environment and harsher penalties against polluters.

Brundtland continues to travel around the world, giving talks on how to heal our endangered planet. She has brought vision to Norway's future. In her own words, "The doctor first tries to prevent illness, then tries to treat it if it comes. It's exactly the same as what you try to do as a politician, but with regard to society."

Julia Chang Bloch

Julia Chang Bloch is the first female ambassador to Nepal. President Bush appointed Bloch to this distant post in 1989, making her one of a handful of U.S. women ambassadors. At first, Bloch thought it would be a relatively quiet appointment because Nepal had a reputation for peacefulness. A few months after her arrival, however, the remote nation nestled at the base of the Himalayas erupted into violence. The Nepalese demonstrated in Katmandu (Nepal's capital) for democracy, protesting the monarchy of King Birendra. April 6, 1990 was a day of bloodshed in Katmandu. Hundreds of thousands of protesters marched on the Royal Palace until the police and army fired into the crowds, killing dozens and wounding hundreds. Bloch found herself protecting more than 1,000 American tourists who were trapped in Nepal. She issued a warning to prevent further visitors from coming to this battle-torn city, and drew up a plan to evacuate the Americans already there. She was able to talk to both King Birendra and the protesters, thereby helping solve the situation. The King was replaced by an interim government, and free elections were scheduled to take place in 1991.

Julia was born in 1943 in China, daughter to Chang Fu-yun, the first Chinese national to earn a law degree from Harvard. In 1951 when the Communists took power, he fled to the United States with his wife and three children.

Chang studied communications and languages as an undergraduate at the University of California at Berkeley. She was inspired by President John F. Kennedy and his creation of the Peace Corps, an agency of skilled volunteers who go to foreign countries to give aid. She taught English as a second language in Malaysia, an experience important to her future career as a diplomat. While studying government and East Asian studies at Harvard, she met Stuart Marshall Bloch, a lawyer. Two years later they were married and moved to Washington D.C., where Julia Chang Bloch worked in the Peace Corps' administration office.

She soon became a personal staff member to Republican Senator Charles Percy, who later made her chief minority counsel of the Senate Select Committee on Nutrition and Human Needs. She headed the U.S. AIDS Food for Peace program in Africa, a famine relief project.

Today, Ambassador Bloch is involved in planning efforts to save Nepal's mountain forests and bring electricity to rural areas. She hopes to assist in future free elections and help draft reforms for the Nepalese Constitution. To the Nepalis, she is not only a representative of U.S. democracy, but also an American of Asian descent who has a good understanding of their needs and hopes.

3 Science And Medicine

In Western society, women were not allowed to enter scientific professions until the late 19th century. And even for these early women scientists, it was an uphill fight. Many were shunned by society. Yet females often made great contributions to astronomy, mathematics, and other sciences.

Women were significant scientists early in history. For example, the first woman mathematician, Hypatia, was born in Alexandria, Egypt. She devoted herself to the study of astronomy, and helped design the astrolabe. Early Christians, however, considered learning and science to be pagan activities, and were suspicious of anyone who practiced them. It was no surprise, then, that an angry mob murdered the gifted Hypatia. Centuries later, in 1815, another brilliant woman mathematician was born. Augusta Ada Byron became known as the first computer programmer. In 1979 a new computer language—Ada—was named after her. Like Hypatia, she died young. But unlike her Egyptian predecessor, Ada left many scientific notes and memoirs.

Only in the 20th century have women overcome social barriers and been allowed to obtain a scientific education. Many have achieved fame such as Dian Fossey and Jane Goodall, who studied the behavior of primates in their natural habitats.

Today women are becoming an ever-increasing percentage of the scientific and medical work force. Thirty-four percent of the 1989 graduates of medical schools in the United States were women, and more women are enrolling in scientific college programs.

There are still biases against women and minority groups, however, that prevent them from reaching top-level jobs. As evidence of this there was only one female medical school dean, 39 science department chairwomen, and 47 clinical department chairwomen in the U.S. in 1989.

Two important women in the field of science, a Nobel Prize winner and the current U.S. Surgeon General, have made significant contributions to the scientific world and increased participation for women in nontraditional professions.

Barbara McClintock

The first woman to win unshared honors in Medicine or Physiology from the Nobel Committee was Barbara McClintock. At age 81, she accepted the award for her discovery of mobile genetic elements. Her discovery—that genes could jump around on chromosomes—is at the basis of today's advances in genetic engineering.

Barbara McClintock was born in 1902 in Hartford, Connecticut. From early childhood she was intrigued with how mechanical objects worked. This interest gave way to studying biology and chemistry in high school. Her parents didn't encourage a college education for their daughter, but they finally allowed her to go to Cornell University's College of Agriculture where she majored in biology. She studied botany in graduate school, where she specialized in genetics. Her lifelong work was devoted to analyzing the genes that make varieties of corn different.

For many years McClintock's greatest discoveries went unnoticed by colleagues in the scientific community. But in the 1970s, she was finally recognized when the genes began to "jump" (as she had predicted decades before) in bacteria, yeast, and the fruit fly. Finally others realized that her research was of fundamental importance. It unlocked the door to

Dr. Barbara McClintock was 81 years old when she finally received the
Nobel Prize in medicine for her work in genetics.

understanding the cause of viral cancer and African sleeping sickness.

In 1979 she won the MacArthur Award for basic research. Three years later she won the Nobel Prize. The Committee called McClintock's work "one of the two great discoveries of our time in genetics." The other was the earlier discovery of the double helix shape of DNA.

Antonia Novello

Antonia Novello was appointed Surgeon General of the United States by President Bush. She has had to fill the shoes of the last Surgeon General, outspoken C. Everett Koop, who gained national attention by promoting sex education and the use of condoms to help prevent the spread of AIDS. Dr. Novello has brought her own concerns into the spotlight. She is concerned about the increasing number of women who contract lung cancer.

Dr. Novello was born in Fajardo, Puerto Rico, and received her doctorate at the University of Puerto Rico School of Medicine in San Juan. She spent her pediatric residency years at the University of Michigan Medical Center, and studied kidney disease at Georgetown University. Novello holds another advanced degree—a Master's in public health from Johns Hopkins School of Hygiene. She has headed up the National Institute of Child Health and Human Development since 1986. Dr. C. Everett Koop gave her an Exemplary Service Medal in 1989.

Novello has established a long commitment to the health of women and children in the United States. Since her appointment as Surgeon General, she has especially targeted smoking, asking that minors not be allowed to buy cigarettes. She has also highlighted the health gains seen in smokers who quit. Novello is not shy about denouncing advertisers who encourage women to smoke by running ads that make smoking seem sophisticated or glamorous.

21

United States Surgeon General Dr. Antonia Novello coordinates government policy regarding health issues.

Another important matter she has addressed is the consumption of alcohol by children. She is outspoken on criticizing beer companies and others who encourage children and adolescents to drink. As Surgeon General, Dr. Antonia Novello will surely make changes in conventional attitudes toward preventive health care in the United States.

4 Spiritual Leaders

In ancient Egypt, perhaps the most important deity was the goddess Isis. She had great powers. According to a 4,000-year-old legend, Isis gathered together the pieces of Osiris, her murdered husband, bringing him back to life. She also protected her son, Horus, from meeting Osiris' fate. Even Anubis, the Egyptian god of death, came under her control. For centuries Isis was worshipped as healer of the sick and bringer of life, both as mother and supernatural goddess.

Women throughout history have played an important role in the formation and history of religion. Astarte, for example, was revered by the Semitic and Mediterranean cultures as the goddess of fertility and reproduction. In the Hebrew Bible, written shortly before the birth of Christ, the account of creation tells how a single woman, Eve, was formed from the body of a single man, Adam, to be his companion.

The most positive and honored of women in recorded history is Mary, mother of Jesus. Centuries later she is still revered, honored, prayed to, and loved by worshippers who try to emulate her purity and goodness.

From ancient times to today, women have been members of the clergy. There have been Buddhist, Protestant, and Catholic nuns, female rabbis and ministers. They have died for their faith. Some, like Mother Cabrini, have been canonized as saints in the Catholic religion. But as in most walks of life, women have not reached positions of power. Women in the Roman Catholic faith cannot become priests, bishops, cardinals, or Pope. Mormon women serve as missionaries but do not ascend to their church's top posts. Similarly, Muslim women do not rise to power within Islam. Despite this, women have been and continue to be honored by their respective faiths and the world as great religious leaders.

Mother Teresa

Mother Teresa's given name is Agnes Gonxha Bojaxhiu. She was born in 1910 to Albanian parents. Drawn to religious life, she entered a Roman Catholic convent when she was a teenager. After becoming a nun, she was sent to Calcutta, India, to teach in a school for upper-class children. Mother Teresa taught there for more than 20 years.

The plight of poor people in Calcutta did not escape her compassionate gaze. Her desire to help them became so strong that she left her order to live among them. In Calcutta she founded the Missionaries of Charity order. She began to distribute food and medicine, and treat the sick and the dying. She founded a leprosy center which resulted in 119 centers across India and around the world. When she was 58 she founded the Coworkers of the Missionaries of Charity, which today has over three million members.

Mother Teresa's mission did not confine itself to the poor of India. She traveled to Rome, London, and— when she was past 60—New York, where she started the first North American mission in a slum of the South Bronx. Her tireless efforts on behalf of the world's poor earned her the Nobel Peace Prize in 1979.

Although she is now past the age of 80, Mother Teresa continues to attend the poor and sick. She has inspired countless followers of various religious beliefs in 71 countries. Hundreds of clinics, schools, hostels for AIDS victims, soup kitchens, and homeless shelters now exist because of her. People all over the world admire her for the love and devotion she gives to others.

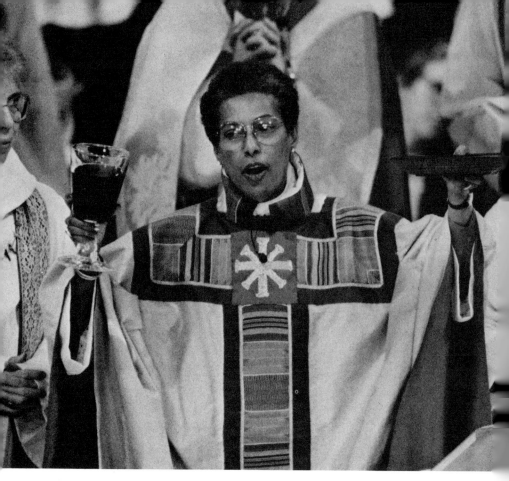

Dr. Barbara Harris of Boston broke a precedent in the 1980s when she became the first female to be ordained bishop in the Episcopal Church.

Barbara Harris

The first female to be ordained bishop in the history of the Episcopal Church is Barbara Harris. In the winter of 1988 the diocese of Massachusetts chose Harris, a black woman, to wear the miter (a headdress worn by bishops and abbots). Many churchgoers and leaders in the Episcopal church were outraged. The Archbishop of Canterbury, worldwide leader of Episcopalians, announced that the church would not recognize her ordination or any clergy she herself would ordain. Many conservatives in the worldwide Anglican community still disapprove of Harris' ordination, even though the American branch officially sanctioned the ordination of women in 1976.

Conservative Episcopalian leaders feel that bishops

are successors to Christ's apostles. They also believe that since none of Jesus' apostles were women, the line of succession is broken when a woman enters the ranks. Further, they feel that any hope of solving the differences between Episcopalians and Roman Catholics is jeopardized by women in the priesthood (Roman Catholics also do not ordain women priests).

On the other hand, Barbara Harris is drawing many people back to the church because she reaches out to both women and minorities. In her own words, she wants to "offer my peculiar gifts as a black woman...a sensitivity and an awareness that come out of more than a speaking acquaintance with oppression."

Harris was born in 1930 in Philadelphia, where her father worked as a steel worker. She grew up in an atmosphere of civil rights awareness. She did not graduate from college or attend the seminary. Instead, she went into public relations where she learned effective argument techniques. By the early 1950s, her voice was heard in the clamor of the civil rights movement. She worked for Sun Oil Company as a public relations officer, and went to Mississippi to help register black voters during summer vacations.

Two years before the U.S. Episcopal church officially admitted women into the priesthood, Harris led a march of 11 women who were illegally ordained in Philadelphia. By 1980 she herself was ordained. Today she is an outspoken Christian leader who is unafraid of speaking out against injustice and discrimination wherever she finds them.

5 Women Educators

I n ancient Egypt, it was thought that women were the dominant sex. They were well educated, owned property, and held jobs and public office. Egypt was well-known for its ruling queens.

Although lack of specific historical records makes it difficult to assess the education of women in many ancient civilizations, we do know a little about women from the social status they held. Ancient Athenian women, for example, were largely uneducated and confined to their homes. Spartan women, in contrast, held equal positions with men both in education and social status. In ancient Rome, the educational picture for women was bleak. Although they held high social rank, women were thought of as imbeciles under the law.

Women in the Middle Ages didn't fare much better. They were treated as second-class citizens and remained uneducated, except for a few in religious orders. This attitude persisted for centuries in Europe, because it was thought unfeminine to be learned.

During the Renaissance, many brilliant female scholars taught at the great universities of Italy and Spain. But in general, the light of education was at its dimmest for women during the 18th century. Not until the Industrial Revolution of the 19th century were women given the opportunity to receive a college education. In the 1830s women's colleges were founded in the United States and England, and better education for females of all ages became acceptable.

An early educator of children was Maria Montessori, an Italian psychiatrist. Her method of teaching concentrated on developing early reading and writing skills in children as well as giving them physical freedom. She opened her first school in Rome in 1907, and trained teachers around the world in the Montessori method for the next 40 years.

Within the past 100 years the role of women in education changed dramatically. Today women comprise approximately two-thirds of the world's teachers. Nearly 40 percent of American college teachers are women. Yet only a few make it to the top levels of the teaching profession to become department chairpersons, academic deans, administrators, or chancellors. Two prominent women, however, have bucked the odds to overcome gender and race discrimination. They have risen to the top of their field.

Donna Shalala

For Donna Shalala, 1987 was an important year. She became the first woman chancellor of the University of Wisconsin in Madison, the fourth largest university in the United States. She had left her post as president of Hunter College in New York City to become chancellor in Wisconsin. Her appointment came as no surprise, as a woman with her extensive background in politics and finance was exactly what the University of Wisconsin needed. She vowed to help both the University and the state grow economically.

Born in the Midwest, Dr. Shalala was brought up in a Lebanese-American household. She earned her degree at the Western College for Women in Oxford, Ohio, and did a two-year stint in the Peace Corps in Iran where she learned to speak Farsi. After that she studied for her doctorate in urban studies at Syracuse University.

Her job resume is also very impressive. Dr. Shalala was recipient of a Guggenheim fellowship, a visiting professor at Yale Law School, and a faculty member at Columbia University. She was also assistant secretary at the U.S. Department of Housing and Urban

Development during the Carter administration. But her most important job was that of treasurer of the Municipal Assistance Corporation, where she worked to bail New York City out of its fiscal crisis.

One of Dr. Shalala's current goals is to make the University of Wisconsin more ethnically integrated. On a campus with only a five percent minority enrollment, this is a challenge. T-shirts on campus proclaim "Make the University of Wisconsin Safe for People of Any Color."

It is Dr. Shalala's belief that students who graduate from the University of Wisconsin will enter a larger, more ethnically diverse "real world," and that preparing students early in life to meet this challenge is important. She also works hard to stamp out racial tensions on campus. She has already increased the number of minority and female faculty. But her main focus is still on politics and finance, which may one day lead her back to government and a cabinet post. For today, however, she remains a great leader in education.

Betty Allen

The executive director for Harlem School of the Arts is Betty Allen, who is also a talented opera star and educator.

She was born Betty Lou Allen on March 17, 1930 in Campbell, Ohio. Her father was a steel worker and her mother a homemaker who earned extra money taking in laundry. When Betty was 11 her mother died, leaving her daughter to care for the home. When looking after her neglectful, drunken father became too heavy a load, Betty went to the Youngstown courthouse and asked the judge to put her up for adoption. Unhappily, Betty was placed with a number of abusive families.

At 14 she moved into the Youngstown YWCA and cleaned houses to earn money. She also attended high school, sang in a choir, and studied Latin and German. Eventually she went on to college, where she majored in

German and sang in the choir and women's glee club. Her German professor recognized Allen's talent and became her mentor. He encouraged her to apply to the Hartford School of Music in Connecticut, which she did. After being accepted, she managed to attend full-time with partial scholarships and money she earned by leading children's music groups.

Not long after graduating from the School of Music she was chosen by Leonard Bernstein to sing in his symphony, *Jeremiah*. In October 1954, she made her debut in the New York City Opera's revival of *Show Boat*. From that point on, Allen's career soared. During the 1970s Allen focused her energy on teaching. She and her social worker husband, Ritten Edward Lee III, supervised an experimental project that brought teenagers from poor backgrounds to the Marlboro Music Festival in Vermont. In 1979 she was picked to direct the Harlem School of the Arts by its founder, Dorothy Maynor.

The Harlem School of the Arts has a varied curriculum: courses in dance, drama, music appreciation, painting, and photography are only a few of the subjects offered. The school gives students from poor backgrounds opportunities they might not otherwise have. Students pay only what they can afford—sometimes only a few cents per class. Allen oversees not only the curriculum, but school policy and fund-raising. In 1988 she was awarded the New York City Women's Project Exceptional Achievement Award. In 1989 she received the American Composers' Alliance Laurel Leaf Award for her work on behalf of education.

Allen firmly believes in education as a way to keep the United States strong: "Education must once more be made a primary concern. Our children are our future." To this goal, Betty Allen dedicates her life.

6 The Business World

The word "business" can refer to many things—law, medicine, finance, publishing, cosmetics, retailing, banking, and even show business. Today more women than ever before are entering the ranks of high-paid executives but their number is still small compared to males. Most women in business tend to cluster at lower-level jobs and have little chance to break through what's known as the "glass ceiling."

The National Association for Female Executives recently found that its average member earned $36,500 a year. According to the U.S. Bureau of Labor Statistics, fewer than three-tenths of one percent of working women earn $78,000 per year or more.

The good news is that overall, the gap between men and women's salaries has been closing over the past two decades. Today women earn approximately 70 percent of men's wages. The bad news is that the gap between salaries of top executive women and men remains wide. In upper-level jobs, women earn only about 42 percent of what men earn. Even so, there are some women who do make a great deal of money.

Sherry Lansing, a top Hollywood executive, reportedly earns $7 million per year. Estee Lauder's cosmetics company took in $1.6 billion in 1988. Diane Sawyer, a television newscaster, earns about $1.5 million a year. In time perhaps the sheer number of women entering management-level jobs will help shrink the salary gap in the coming years.

Jill Elikann Barad

At 39, Jill Elikann Barad ranks among the highest

paid women executives in the United States. She is president of Mattel Toys, the company that manufactures the Barbie doll. In 1989 Barad earned around $614,000.

Barad was born in New York to parents active in the arts: Her mother was an artist and her father a television director. Both parents encouraged Barad to become whatever she wanted to be. While attending Queens College, she worked as a beauty consultant for Love Cosmetics. Later she became production assistant to movie producer Dino De Laurentiis. She married Thomas Barad, an executive at Paramount Pictures, and moved to Los Angeles. She began working for Mattel in 1981, as a product manager and quickly climbed the corporate ladder.

Promoting Barbie's success is just one of Barad's accomplishments. She also created the Magic Nursery doll, which became an immediate hit in the toy world. Barad is a marketing whiz. She came up with the idea of the "Barbie Summit" in 1990 to give Barbie a socially conscious image. Held in New York, the summit gathered together 40 children from 28 countries who attended workshops on the problems facing today's world. The children decided that their number one concern was peace. Mattel donated $500,000 to different agencies that promote world peace.

Cathleen Black

As publisher of the newspaper USA Today, Cathleen Black earns approximately $600,000 a year. Traditionally publishing doesn't pay well, but for a few executives at the top, a hefty salary can be earned.

Cathleen Prunty Black grew up in Chicago. Her family loved and encouraged ideas and reading. The youngest of three, Cathy remembers attending parties in her home where current events, art, business, and politics were discussed.

After attending Trinity College in Washington, D.C.,

Katharine Graham—another leader in the publishing world—is head of the powerful media company that owns the influential *Washington Post* newspaper.

she went to New York where she worked in advertising sales for Curtis Publishing. She was on the advertising staff for both *Travel & Leisure* and *New York* magazines. When *Ms.* magazine began publication in 1972, Black was asked to become its first advertising manager. Later she became associate publisher.

By 1977 Black had moved back to New York magazine as associate publisher to help pull it out of financial decline. In 1984 she became publisher of *USA Today*, a job most people in publishing considered risky. But the risk paid off. By 1987 *USA Today* was the most widely read newspaper in the country, with an estimated readership of 5.5 million.

Ms. magazine named Black one of its 1988 Women of the Year. In 1989 she was honored with the Sara Lee Frontrunner Award, given to women of outstanding achievement in the fields of government, business, the arts, and the humanities.

A key to success, Black offers, is a sense of humor: "Humor is a great gift because it is a great weapon. It deflects hostility, tension, anger."

7 The Literary Arts

Women have always played an important role in the history of literature. Jane Austen, for example, is generally acknowledged to be one of the finest writers who ever lived. Her novel *Pride and Prejudice* is one of the greatest novels of all time. George Eliot, whose real name was Mary Ann Evans, was one of the most important writers of the mid-19th century. Virginia Woolf was a master of originality in 20th century literature. Yet women have never been given their due.

In the 90-year history of the Nobel Prize, women have won the prize for literature only six times. Only 20 American women have won Pulitzer prizes for fiction, and just eight female playwrights for drama in 73 years. Women, however, have hardly been absent from the world of letters.

Dame Agatha Christie wrote *The Murder of Roger Ackroyd* in 1926—the biggest-selling novel ever published. Her play *The Mousetrap* has had a London stage run of more than 30 years. Beatrix Potter wrote the best-selling children's book of all time: *The Tale of Peter Rabbit*. The first major work of science fiction, *Frankenstein*, was written in 1818 by Mary Shelley, daughter of 19th century feminist Mary Wollstonecraft. Ursula LeGuin is one of the most popular science fiction authors today. A woman even made the best-seller list when she was over 90: Helen Hooven Santmyer, author of *...And Ladies of the Club*.

Nelly Sachs

Nelly Sachs joined the ranks of Nobel laureates at

age 76 when she received the Prize for Literature. A poet and dramatist who wrote about the plight of Jews in Nazi Germany, Sachs was an eloquent spokesperson for Holocaust survivors. She memorialized their sufferings in plays such as *Eli: A Mystery Play of the Sufferings of Israel.*

Born in 1891 in Berlin, Germany, Sachs was the daughter of a wealthy manufacturer and inventor. Her writing career began while she was just in her teens, trying her hand at poetry.

After the Nazis took power in Germany, Sachs' life was in grave danger. She was almost sent to a concentration camp, but escaped with the help of friend Selma Lagerlof, with whom she had corresponded. Although they never met, Selma Lagerlof interceded with the Swedish Royal Family to help obtain Sachs' release from Germany. She and her mother fled to Sweden where they lived in a one-room apartment and learned Swedish. Sachs began translating German poetry into Swedish and writing her own poetry again. She reflected on the suffering and death of six million fellow Jews in Germany's concentration camps.

In 1947 a book of her poems was published. One poem, "O the Chimneys," a lament for her dead Jewish brethren, garnered international respect. Her second volume of poetry, *And No One Knows How to Go On*, was published in 1957. It was about reconciliation with God.

Twenty years after she left, Nelly Sachs returned to Germany to accept a prestigious literary award. Two years later, the city of Dortmund, Germany, established an annual literary prize in her name. They also gave her a lifetime pension.

Danielle Steel

Danielle Steel is one of today's best-selling authors of romance fiction. In just 17 years she has published 27 novels— approximately one every six months. Each book makes it to the top of the best-seller list.

Although she died in 1976, Dame Agatha Christie is still the world's best-selling mystery novelist, with more than 300 books sold worldwide in more than 100 languages.

Sometimes she has several novels on the list at a time. Her books are translated into 28 languages, and her annual income is estimated at $25 million.

If writing doesn't keep her busy enough, Steel also has her husband, nine children and four dogs. She is a "participating" mother who drives her children to doctors' appointments, sports events, and recitals.

Her lifestyle today contrasts with that of her parents, who were divorced when Danielle was seven. Nannies and maids reared young Danielle as she spent a lonely but privileged childhood. Her father was a member of the German Lowenbrau family, and her mother the daughter of a Portuguese diplomat. She attended school in Paris and New York, studying fashion design. For a time she worked for a public relations agency in New York where she wrote articles and poetry.

Finally a client spotted her skill with words, and encouraged her to try her hand at writing a novel. Steel moved to San Francisco and wrote that novel, selling it in 1974 for $3,500 to Simon and Schuster. In 1977 she sold her second novel, and she has been producing a constant stream of novels ever since. Steel is boundlessly energetic, requiring only a few hours of sleep a night. This leaves her more time for writing her books on a manual typewriter in her tiny home office.

Although literary critics don't see Steel's novels as great literature, they all agree that she gives her audience the stories they want to read. Her novels are Cinderella-type stories, where every heroine or hero triumphs at the book's end.

Steel enjoys the privacy of her home and family. Enormously successful and sought after by press and fans, she remains shy, shunning the limelight as much as possible. And though many people envy her lifestyle, they don't envy the brutal time schedule she has to keep to satisfy her publishers and readers. She is extremely well-disciplined, hard-working, and serious about her work.

Wendy Wasserstein

Born October 18, 1950, in Brooklyn, New York, Wendy Wasserstein was the youngest of four children. Her father was a successful textile manufacturer, and her mother a homemaker who was interested in theater. Wendy attended Mount Holyoke College, where she thought about becoming a lawyer, but a summer course in playwriting at Smith College changed her mind. Instead, she earned a master's degree in creative writing from City College of New York.

Greatly interested in theater, she then enrolled in the Yale School of Drama, where she earned her Master of

Alice Walker won the Pulitzer Prize for her novel *The Color Purple*, which was made into a movie in 1985.

Fine Arts degree. More important than the degree, however, was the opportunity to associate with many talented, budding playwrights.

While at Yale, Wasserstein wrote a one-act play called *Uncommon Women and Others* which she later expanded. This play, depicting how the women's movement affected students at an exclusive girls' college, became her first off-Broadway success. She went on to write *Isn't It Romantic*, another play exploring women's lives.

In 1986 she began work on *The Heidi Chronicles*, which won the Pulitzer Prize in 1988. It opens with the monologue of Heidi Holland, an art historian who chronicles how women in art have been utterly neglected and ignored by their male contemporaries. The rest of the play is told in flashback and tells not only the personal story of Heidi, but of the women's movement. It spans the movement from consciousness-raising groups to demonstrations, freedom of choice in birth control, sexual choice, AIDS, and single parenting.

Many more plays tackling controversial subjects will surely flow from Wasserstein's pen. She is a board member of Playwrights Horizons, a contributing editor to *New York Woman* magazine, and author of a collection of essays entitled *Bachelor Girls*.

8 The Musical Arts

Murals in Thebes dating back to the year 1500 show female musicians entertaining at festive gatherings. Women played the instruments of their time, sang, and danced. Roman and Greek pottery and murals also show women playing musical instruments. Paintings of Saint Cecilia, a Roman noblewoman who lived in the third century A.D., show her playing the organ.

It wasn't until the 16th century, however, that the first music conservatory for girls was founded in Italy. But little of the earliest Western music was written by women. Perhaps one reason is that much of it was created only for religious ceremonies. Since women were not in charge of the early Christian church, their opportunity for creating music was very limited. One notable exception was Hildegard von Bingen, a cloistered nun in 11th century Germany. She composed a piece of music called "Ordo virtutum" to be sung by 16 female voices.

Not until the 20th century, however, did women begin to make a dent in the male-dominated world of music. Today women performers have international stature in classical music, including Jacqueline du Pre, cellist; Nadia Salerno-Sonnenberg, violinist; Katia and Marielle Labeque, pianists; and Sarah Caldwell, conductor. There are hundreds more.

Within other musical traditions—jazz, folk, rhythm and blues, rock—20th century women have also made their mark. Jazz singers like Bessie Smith, Billie Holiday, Dinah Washington and Ella Fitzgerald helped lead the way for other women to carve a niche in the music world. Joan Baez, folk composer and singer, expressed the political and social feelings of the '60s and '70s. Aretha Franklin, Tina Turner, Madonna, Paula Abdul, and scores of other female performers have sold millions of recordings. They top the charts in sales and popularity, making them as successful as their male counterparts.

Midori

Hailed as perhaps the most dazzling violinist of our time, Midori is a 19-year-old talent who never gets stage fright, except when she has to deliver an oral report in school. She took the musical world by storm when she made a guest appearance at the renowned Tanglewood Music Festival in July 1986. During her performance of Bernstein's "Serenade for Violin and String Orchestra," the E-string on her violin broke. She promptly exchanged her violin for that of the first violinist. When that E-string broke, she calmly traded with another violinist and, without further ado, completed the difficult piece. The audience, orchestra, and conductor Leonard Bernstein all gave her a standing ovation.

Midori Goto was born in Osaka, Japan, on October 25, 1971. Her father is an engineer, and her mother, Setsu Goto, a concert violinist. From the age of two Midori was thrilled by the sounds of the violin. She often attended her mother's rehearsals. Setsu gave her daughter a tiny violin of her own for her third birthday. By age six, Midori gave her first public recital. She practiced several hours each day, usually in an empty room in the concert hall where her mother rehearsed. One day, an American colleague of Setsu overheard Midori playing, tape-recorded the event, and presented it to Dorothy DeLay, a violin teacher at the Juilliard School in New York. As a result, 10-year-old Midori made her debut in 1981 at the Aspen Music Festival, astonishing all who heard her. Violinist Pinchas Zukerman asked Midori to play for his master class at

Aspen, and the experience brought "tears to his eyes."

At age 11, Midori moved to New York with her mother to attend Juilliard. During her first year, Zubin Mehta, music director of the New York Philharmonic, had her perform as surprise soloist in concert on New Year's Eve. She again received a standing ovation.

Midori has appeared in concerts all over the world: in Canada with the Toronto Symphony in 1985; in Japan for the 40th anniversary of the bombing of Hiroshima; and in England with the London Symphony. She has also performed in Germany, France, Austria, and Monaco. In May 1989 she made her official New York orchestral debut with the New York Philharmonic, playing Dvorak's "Concerto in A Minor." Critics describe her technique as breathtaking, and her style as poised, graceful, and dramatic.

Fluent in both her native language and English, Midori considers herself a "New Yorker." Besides her daily practice of violin, she studies karate and writing. Midori also writes a column for a Japanese teen magazine about life in the United States.

Japan is proud of their native daughter. In 1988 she was named Best Artist of the Year—the youngest person to ever receive the honor.

Bonnie Raitt

1990 was a special year for Bonnie Raitt: She won four Grammy Awards. What made it even more special was the fact that she was on top after a career slump. Her record company, Warner Brothers, had dropped her name from its roster four years before. It was the 1989 release of her 10th album "Nick of Time" that made her a star.

Born in Burbank, California, on November 8, 1949, Bonnie was the middle child of three. Music has a history in Raitt's family. Her father is well-known Broadway singer and actor John Raitt, and her mother is his piano accompanist. Raitt's grandfather, a

Methodist missionary, composed 600 hymns and was proficient in playing the Hawaiian slide guitar.

Raitt was brought up as a Quaker. She attended Quaker summer camps where she listened to the music played by camp counselors, including the first songs of the counter-culture peace movement. The lyrics of Joan Baez and Pete Seeger also inspired her. Later in her career she combined her musical talent with her commitment to social change. Raitt taught herself guitar by imitating blues guitarists. After attending a Quaker high school in New York, Raitt went to Radcliffe College where she majored in African studies. In her spare time she practiced guitar. After college, she performed at small clubs in Philadelphia and Cambridge. By 1971 she had met many of the blues artists whose styles she had copied. They already considered her a peer because of her talent.

In 1971 Raitt recorded her first album for Warner Brothers. It included the hit single that would speak for the feminist cause: "Women Be Wise." During the '70s she released many albums, none of which were commercial successes. But she gained a loyal following and high praise from critics. Deeply concerned with ecology, she joined Musicians United for Safe Energy, a political group founded by Jackson Browne, Graham Nash, John Hall, and others. During the 1980s Raitt was active in such causes as Farm Aid, Amnesty International, and the anti-apartheid movement. When her 1986 album "Nine Lives" didn't do well, Warner Brothers dropped her. Later she signed with Capitol Records and recorded "Nick of Time," which became a huge success. The record went platinum and earned her four Grammy awards.

Now that Raitt has her life back on track, she continues to devote time to worthy causes. In a 1990 *Rolling Stone* profile she told interviewer James Henke, "Music's great, but what's important is doing something meaningful with your life."

9 Superb Athletes

S ports have afforded women and minority groups opportunities not offered in other career pursuits. For example, tennis player Althea Gibson was the first black woman to break the color barrier in women's tennis. Gibson traveled a long way from the streets of Harlem where she played paddle tennis, basketball, and volleyball with the neighborhood boys. In 1950 at age 23 she won the U.S. National Championship. At 24 she won Wimbledon.

In 1960 another American black woman overcame great odds, including polio in childhood, to become a sports leader. Wilma Rudolph won three gold medals at the Olympics for track and field.

Earlier in this century Norway's Sonja Henie included ballet training in her figure skating to change the sport forever. She won gold medals for skating in the 1928, 1932, and 1936 Olympics, then went on to motion picture fame as an actress.

These are just three women who have led the way for a host of talented female athletes to excel in the modern era. Until a few decades ago, sports were the province of "gentlemen." Today, while male athletes still dominate much of the sporting scene (football, basketball, baseball and boxing remain closed to females), women have carved niches in other athletic events, and will continue to do so.

Janet Evans

On September 21, 1988, a teenager won the Olympic Gold medal for the women's 400-meter freestyle swimming event. Her name is Janet Evans. In all, she won three Olympic Gold medals in swimming and seven national titles (an American record). She was also named American Female Swimmer of 1988. But instead of endorsing commercial products for a lot of money, Evans chose to finish high school and compete in college athletics. In other words, Evans was more interested in competing and getting an education than she was in making a fast fortune.

Placentia, California, was the birthplace of Janet Evans in 1971. She is the youngest of three children. Her father is a veterinarian and her mother a homemaker. Janet started swimming when she was two years old. Her parents and brothers encouraged her in her pursuit of swimming, but did not pressure her into competition. Her love of the water was obvious. While in elementary school she began practicing with the local swim club, then joined the Fullerton Aquatic Sports Team. Her first swimming milestone came when she was 10: she set a national age group record in the 200-yard freestyle.

By age 14 Evans came close to making the World Championship team in the 800-meter and 1,500-meter freestyle. She won two bronze medals in the 1986 Goodwill Games in Moscow. Then in 1987 she won three national titles in the 400-, 800-, and 1,500-meter freestyle. That same year she was also chosen as U.S. Swimmer of the Year.

Besides being a very disciplined athlete who trains according to a rigorous schedule, Evans is also a well-rounded human being who values family, friends, and a good education. She believes that these, along with her ability and hard work, are the keys to success.

Arantxa Sanchez Vicario

In the summer of 1989, Arantxa (pronounced ah-RAHN-cha) Sanchez Vicario upset top-ranked Steffi Graf in the French Open women's tennis finals. It catapulted her into the limelight and moved her

Arantxa Sanchez holds the victory cup after defeating Steffi Graf in the final of the 1989 French Open.

standing in competitive tennis from 18th to fifth. She became the first Spanish woman to ever win a Grand Slam event. The thrill of victory brought another perk: an invitation from Spain's King Juan Carlos and Queen Sofia for Arantxa and her parents to the royal palace in Madrid. As Sanchez Vicario tells it, "The King tells me how he was watching me on TV and cheering 'Come on. Go, Arantxa.' Can you imagine? The King! I didn't know kings did things like that."

Arantxa Sanchez Vicario was born in 1973 in Madrid, Spain. When she was two, her family moved to Barcelona. They lived near the Club Real de Tenis, where the whole family took up the sport. Instead of playing with dolls, Arantxa followed her parents, older brothers and sister onto the tennis court. Since all of them became top-ranked players, it was only natural for Arantxa to become Spain's top-ranked female. When she was only 14 she turned pro. Coached by Juan Nunez, the Chilean pro, she nearly upset the great Martina Navratilova.

As is the case with many athletes, Sanchez Vicario follows a rigorous training schedule that doesn't allow for much socializing. Until after she won the French Open, she had never even been inside a disco. Filled with energy, she expends most of it practicing, competing and, in her spare time, playing with her two dogs Roland and Crac. Sometimes she relaxes in a restaurant on the Ramblas, a promenade on Barcelona's seaport.

For a woman filled with boundless energy, however, she probably won't be able to relax too long. There are too many titles to be won. In her words, "tennis is a funny little ride. If you don't practice and you don't want to play, you go down. But me, I run all the balls and really enjoy playing."

That's what makes her a winner.

10 Military And Law Enforcement

Women make up 8.8 percent of the U.S. Navy, 10.5 percent of the Army, and 12.5 percent of the Air Force. And their numbers continue to increase. For example, on the San Diego-based destroyer *Cape Cod*, nearly 40 percent of the 1,200-member crew is female. Women in the armed forces are trained the same as men and are eligible for the same jobs and promotions. They are barred by law from combat, however. Until Congress decides to change that law, future opportunities for service women will continue to be limited to noncombat operations.

Until recently, police forces in the United States also barred women from "line-of-fire" positions. They were employed mainly as meter maids, secretaries, and clerks. Today, however, women make up about 13 percent of the American police force, serving alongside men as detectives and "beat cops." It is no longer unusual to see a woman policeman out on patrol.

The women described below are true leaders. One is a brigadier general, and the other a big-city police chief. They are outstanding role models for women interested in military and law enforcement occupations.

Gail Reals

Gail Reals was the highest-ranking woman in the U.S. Marines, and the first woman to become a commanding general of a marine base. For two years Brigadier General Reals oversaw the base in Quantico, Virginia, where she had responsibility for 9,000 students, enlistees, officers, and civilian employees. She retired in June 1990 at the age of 54.

Reals did not have a privileged upbringing. She was born near Syracuse, New York, where her mother worked as a maid and her father as a welder. When he died, Gail was 14 years old. To help with family finances, she took a job as a live-in baby-sitter. When she graduated from high school, she worried that she would work forever in an low-paying job, so she joined the Marines.

After basic training, she spent several years as a stenographer in the secretarial pool. In 1968 she received a commission as second lieutenant, and began to advance through the ranks in a series of command jobs. In 1968 she went to Beirut, Lebanon, as personnel officer in the Marine security guard battalion. During the 1970s she was commanding officer of the Woman Recruit Training Battalion at Paris Island, South Carolina. By 1985 she was promoted to the rank of general by President Reagan.

When asked how she felt about performing a man's job, Reals responded, "I don't think to be professional I have to be more masculine. I'm not a very good imitation man."

Elizabeth Watson

In February 1990 Elizabeth Watson was sworn in as police chief of Houston, Texas, the country's fourth largest city. Although other women have served as police chiefs in other cities —notably Penny Harrington of Portland, Oregon—none has headed a major city's police force. Watson commands nearly 4,000 officers, 90 percent of them male. She began by making much-needed changes. For example, the starting salary for Houston police officers was among the lowest in the nation's top 20 cities. She quickly raised their salaries by six percent.

Elizabeth Herrmann was born to parents who encouraged her to excel. Her father was a NASA aerospace engineer, and her mother had many relatives

Houston Police Chief Elizabeth Watson is one of several high-profile women in law enforcement nationwide.

on the Philadelphia Police Force. Mrs. Herrmann had been inspired by stories her father and brothers told, and passed them along to her two daughters. Both went into police work. Elizabeth's sister became the first woman captain of the Harris County, Texas, Sheriff's Department.

Elizabeth joined the Houston Police Department in 1973, and has worked in a dozen different divisions including juvenile, jail, SWAT, burglary, homicide, and auto theft. Many assignments involved dangerous moments when she had to arrest burglars, rapists, and murderers.

In 1976 she married Robert Watson, a sergeant in the Houston Police Department who doesn't mind that his wife outranks him. He is an investigator who also does most of the grocery shopping. The Watsons have a successful working partnership that both of them enjoy.

Watson's typical day as Police Chief involves talking to city council members and touring local stations to meet with officers under her jurisdiction. She also talks to elementary school students about drugs, and local citizen's groups about drug abuse and crimes against women.

Chief Watson says her main priority is "to push decision making downward, to make the department less bureaucratic and semi-military." She also enjoys serving as a role model for women in police work—a profession she considers both challenging and rewarding.

11 The Environment

Perhaps the reason voters consider ecology to be a campaign issue of women candidates is that the modern prophet of the environmental movement is Rachel Carson. In 1962 Carson published the landmark book *Silent Spring*, in which she attacked the use of pesticides. Eight years later an environmental agency banned the use of the legal pesticide DDT.

Women continue to crusade on behalf of the environment throughout the world. Many notables work hard to preserve our fragile planet, including Dorene Bolze, a policy analyst for the New York Audubon Society. She coordinates the Citizen's Acid Rain Monitoring Network and pushes for legislation to reduce sources of pollution.

Janet Patricia Gibson, a botanist/zoologist from Belize, helped create the Hol Chan reserve to help preserve the fragile ecosystem. Lois Gibbs made headlines in her battle to have the town of Love Canal near Niagara Falls declared toxic because chemical waste had seeped into the groundwater. Love Canal was evacuated, and Gibbs went to Washington, D.C. to head up the Citizens Clearinghouse for Hazardous Wastes. Women today are playing a big role in helping save our planet.

Marjory Stoneman Douglas

Marjory Stoneman Douglas has fought for more than 70 years to save Florida's Everglades. In 1927 a committee was established to help create a national park within the Everglades. She was on the original committee and, in a sense, still is. More than 50 awards

Rachel Carson was a pioneer in the movement toward
environmental awareness.

have honored Douglas for trying to save the Everglades. She even has a building named after her: The Department of Natural Resources in Tallahassee, Florida.

Born in Minneapolis in 1890, Douglas was reared in New England. Her parents divorced when she was just six, and her father moved to Florida where he practiced law and later published the *News Record*, Miami's first daily newspaper.

After attending Wellesley College, she married Kenneth Douglas, a newspaper editor. Their union was an unhappy one, however, and they divorced. It was then that she went to Florida and reestablished a strong relationship with her father, a man passionately interested in Florida's geography.

For 15 years, Marjory Douglas worked as a magazine writer, eventually writing a book about the Everglades. The task was huge, taking Douglas five years to complete. *The Everglades, or River of Grass*, received an enthusiastic reception, and has not been out of print since its 1947 publication. Despite her efforts to save the Everglades, however, it has now lost half its bird population and much of its water has been drained for towns and farmland. Douglas continues to fight to preserve the 100-mile long Everglades.

The Everglades isn't Douglas' only cause. She's also written about the plight and bad treatment of migrant workers. Her interest in nature resulted in her crusades to protect the coral reefs off Key Largo, the endangered panther, and the wood stork. She has also written her autobiography. At over 100 years of age, she is currently working on a biography of W.H. Hudson, an earlier naturalist whom she greatly admired.

Sara Parkin

A former co-secretary of the European Greens, Sara Parkin calls herself an "ordinary person and party speaker" who spreads the message of world ecology. The Greens, a British party founded in 1973, lobbies for a radical overhaul of the world ecology and economy. But their membership and message are not limited to Great Britain.

"Greens" are active all over Western Europe and Scandinavia. They hold seats in several government legislatures. Greens advocate peace, ecology, and redistribution of the wealth. Outspoken and caring, Sara Parkin has become a visible proponent of Greens issues.

Sara McKewan was born in 1946 in Aberdeen, Scotland, to a middle-class family. Her family moved to England where her father set up his medical practice. Like her father, Sara chose to enter the medical profession. She studied nursing in Scotland at the Edinburgh Royal Infirmary. There she met her future husband, Max Parkin, a doctor.

Sara had read a lot about an issue that deeply concerned her: ecology. She also learned an invaluable lesson from her dying patients. They taught her the importance of accomplishing as much as she could during her lifetime so she would have no regrets when her time came. She also became inspired by lectures given by the late C. H. Waddington, a retired professor, who spoke of limiting industrial growth. Most people thought building and industry always meant progress, but Waddington said it meant just the opposite. He believed that halting this so-called "progress" was not only possible, but the only choice for a planet in fragile health.

Parkin continues to enjoy an international reputation as a Greens' advocate. In August 1990 she traveled to Prague to discuss environmental programs with the Czechoslovakian government, and to Rome to speak to a group of NATO training officers. Perhaps one day she will sit in Parliament. Until that time comes, she will continue to dedicate herself to the "greening" of Europe and the world.

Conclusion

There is a rising tide of women around the world who are entering previously male-dominated careers. Their numbers will continue to increase. As our world becomes more complex and technologically advanced, it becomes more difficult to think of women as the weaker or lesser sex. It takes only a glimpse at statistics on aging to see that women are definitively not weaker: they generally live longer than men and are more resistant to disease.

Over the last 25 years our attitudes toward women and their roles have changed dramatically. They will continue to change. In many countries it is no longer legal or socially acceptable to discriminate against women. People are coming to understand that a human being's place in society must be based on individual achievement rather than gender.

Perhaps in the next few decades women will become so thoroughly integrated into every level of society that a book on their achievements, like this one, will no longer be necessary. As the writer Virginia Woolf once wrote, "...it is fatal to be a man or woman pure and simple; one must be woman-manly or man-womanly."

Glossary

CULTURAL STEREOTYPING. The unwritten rules of a society that put labels on people regardless of their talents or abilities.

ECOLOGY. The study of the interaction between living things and their environment.

EQUAL RIGHTS AMENDMENT (ERA). The amendment to the Constitution that failed to get ratification from enough states. The amendment proposed that equality would not be denied on the basis of sex.

FEMINISM. The philosophy of political, economic, and social equality of the sexes.

"GLASS CEILING." The invisible barrier that impedes women's progress in the business world and education.

MATERNITY LEAVE. A period of time when women take time off from their jobs to have a baby and care for it in infancy. In the U.S., a common maternity leave from a job is six weeks. Sometimes an employer pays for part of the time off.

NOBEL PRIZE. A yearly prize given in various categories (mathematics, science, literature, peace, medicine) to people who work for the interests of humanity.

Bibliography

Books

Blau, Justine. *Betty Friedan*. New York: Chelsea House Publishers, 1990.

Rix, Sara E., ed. *The American Woman 1990-1991*. New York: W.W. Norton & Company, 1990.

Tuttle, Lisa. *Heroines*. London: Harrap Limited, 1988.

Daffron, Carolyn. *Gloria Steinem*. New York: Chelsea House Publishers, 1988.

Periodicals

Allis, Tim. "While looking for a few good men, the Marines found Gail Reals; generally speaking, they're satisfied." *People Weekly*, October 24, 1988: 109-110.

Angelou, Maya. "History-Making in Print." *Savvy Woman*, October 1989: 83.

Boudreau, Richard. "The Great Conciliator." *Los Angeles Times Magazine*, January 6, 1991: 9-13; 30-33.

Brooks, Nancy Rivera. "Barbie's Doting Sister." *Los Angeles Times*, December 10, 1990: D4-5.

Carey, Joseph. "Denominational Gender Gap." *U.S. News & World Report*, June 19, 1989: 56-57.

Carlisle, Kim. "Janet Evans: Good As Gold." *Women's Sports & Fitness,* April, 1989: 28-32.

Chua-Eoan, Howard G. "All in the Family." *Time Special Issue, Women: The Road Ahead,* Fall 1990: 33-34.

Cohen, Sherry Suib. "Beyond Macho: Cathleen Black." *Working Woman,* February 1989: 82.

Crook, Barbara Hustedt. "Cosmo Talks to Elizabeth Watson: Houston's pioneering police chief." *Cosmopolitan,* October 1990: 116; 180.

Current Biography. Edited by Charles Moritz, vol. 51, no. 6, June 1990: 32-35.

"Defenders of the Planet." *Time,* April 23, 1990: 78-79.

Fisher, Anne B. "The 10 Best-Paid Women in America." *Savvy Woman,* July / August 1990: 44-51.

Fritsch, Jane. "Women Making Waves in Navy." *Los Angeles Times,* April 9, 1989: Sec. I, 3.

Gibbs, Nancy. "Radical Daughter: Gro Harlem Brundtland." *Time,* September 25, 1989: 42-43.

Gladstone, Valeria. "Marjory Stoneman Douglas." *Ms.,* January/February 1989: 68-71.

Goldman, Jane. "A Few Good Women." *Savvy Woman,* January 1989: 60-63.

Gross, Liza L. "Dr. Antonia Novello: The Right Stuff. *Hispanic,* January/February 1990: 20.

Infusino, Divina. "Talent At Work: Jill Barad." *Harper's*

Bazaar, March 1990: 184-185; 246.

Istona, Mildred. "Would Women Govern Differently?" *Chatelaine ,* October 1988: 4.

Lichtenstein, Grace. "Witness to Freedom." *Savvy Woman,* July/August 1990: 56-59; 81.

Lidz, Franz. "Tennis With Plenty Of Bounce." *Sports Illustrated,* May 14, 1990: 10-13.

Master, Kim. "It's How You Play The Game." *Working Woman,* May 1990: 88-90.

McElwaine, Sandra. "Danielle Steel: Supermom, Superwife, Superauthor." *Woman's Day,* January 16, 1990: 102-103; 127; 141.

Preston, Mark. "Arantxa Sanchez: Still the Same, Only Better." *Tennis,* January 1990: 32-36.

Rosellini, Lynn. "The First of the 'Mitered Mamas'." *U.S. News & World Report,* June 19, 1989: 56-57.

Stead, Deborah. "The Greening of Sara Parkin." *Savvy Woman,* November 1990: 64-67; 88; 90.

Van Gelder, Lindsy. "Tackling the Big Ten." *Savvy Woman,* December 1989: 72-76; 104.

Index

About The Author

Cecilia Fannon grew up in New York City. She has written screenplays for television, plays for theatre, and has published short stories in an anthology called Flash Fiction. Her hobbies are tap dancing, drawing, and studying foreign languages. She makes her home in Newport Beach, California, with her husband, Jonathan Bliss, and cat, Charley Kitten.